Humming the Thing

poems by

Theresa Hamman

Finishing Line Press
Georgetown, Kentucky

Humming the Thing

Copyright © 2021 by Theresa Hamman
ISBN 978-1-64662-566-6 First Edition
All rights reserved under International and Pan-American Copyright Conventions. No part of this book may be reproduced in any manner whatsoever without written permission from the publisher, except in the case of brief quotations embodied in critical articles and reviews.

ACKNOWLEDGMENTS

Poems previously published from this collection include the following:

"Halo Flash" and "The Wrong Companion" in *The Tower Journal*
"Crows" and "Ear Worm" in *Red Wheelbarrow Review*
"Point Lobos" in *The Paddock Review*
"A Mind without a Bird," "Tuesday, Rural Oregon, In September" and "The Afterlife Is a Dining Car" in *Atomic Flyswatter*
"She" in *Red Hyacinth*

Publisher: Leah Huete de Maines
Editor: Christen Kincaid
Cover Art: Josie Muth
Author Photo: Theresa Hamman
Cover Design: Elizabeth Maines McCleavy

Order online: www.finishinglinepress.com
also available on amazon.com

Author inquiries and mail orders:
Finishing Line Press
PO Box 1626
Georgetown, Kentucky 40324
USA

Table of Contents

Ear Worm 1

She 2

A Mind without a Bird 6

Crows 7

Rural Oregon. Tuesday. In September 9

What Now For April? 10

Cleaning Out the Childhood Closet 11

Trimming the Rose Bushes 1973 13

Birth Day—Part One 15

The Afterlife Is a Dining Car 16

Binary 19

She—Continued 20

Marked 21

Night Shift Musing in the Desert Southwest—Circa 1995 22

Birth Day—Part Two 24

Urgent Prayers 25

Golgotha 26

Halo Flash 27

Point Lobos 29

The Wrong Companion 30

Psalm 23 31

Brief Hope 32

For Abby:

Radiant hope. Radiant love. You are the new dawn, the new sun. You are light.

Ear Worm

I'm at the stage
where I'm humming the thing

between lip and lung
my breathy tongue

slips and curls under the tune
without woodwinds
or throat, or sparrows.

It winds up my brain
slithers out my ear,
weeps down my cheek.

All the while
my mouth
remains tight

and the worm,
finding the small gap
between my teeth,

sings free

She

1. Dress Up

She watches
her sister play dress
up in a mirror
glued to a pink jewelry box,
a ballerina spinning
to broken music,
rouge on her cheeks, nose,
eyelids caked blue,
shiny cotton candy lips,
strings
of pearls cascading down,
a fur stole draped
over her shoulders.
Even absurd,
her sister is Daddy's princess.

2. Hunters

She and the boy
who thinks she's a boy
load caps into toy guns.
She shoots him—
he dies. He
says his dad will take
him hunting this year.
She lies,
says mine will too.
He sits up,
shoots her.
She falls over dead.

3. Stay-Put Sponge Curlers

Her mother
tries different things
to take the boy out—

hair net, Dippity Dew,
stay-put sponge curlers.

By morning, the curlers
end up on her pillow.
Her mother sighs,
lets her wear jeans to school.

4. Clouds

Saturday dawns wet
she lies in dew.
The sun stains the clouds red,
sponges absorbing fire. She
watches them form horses,
aliens, dragons.

"God, why don't you fix me?"

The grass soaks
her clothes, her hair.
Overhead the dragon's
teeth drips and the sun
explodes from its maw.

She pulls herself up, stands,
watches the volcano
become the bleeding
chest of a woman.

God's answer: she will remain a girl.

5. Church

She wears a red dress
to church, covers
her ears
against the organ's rusty song,
the screeching choir voices.
They sound entombed,
and she thinks about tombs,
about resurrection—

Mary Magdalene's stark red
hair on stained glass,
Christ's blood tracks
down his chipped face
His eyes, hands
gone, only scarlet nails
remain in the rotting wood.
She looks for holes
in her own palms.

The priest drones on about
man being made in God's
image. She stares
at the beautiful Mary Magdalene.

No wonder Jesus loved her.

6. Apples and Their Trees

After church
she sprawls on a high tree limb,
thinks about the cross,
the dogwood that birthed it.
At the end of each petal, nail prints.

The wind sways the limb
and her bare feet dangle
over the leaves.
She bites an apple and juice runs
down her chin.
A worm crawls out
she puts it on her chest.

The sky roils with clouds.

Winds blow her mother into view.

A storm comes.

As the limb tries to buck her off,
the lattice above her shifts,
and the red fabric blows
up to her face,
bathes everything crimson.

The apple's juice
on her palms,
sweet stigmata,
she licks it off and
drops the apple core.

It lands at her mother's feet.

A Mind Without a Bird

The coffee brews
whether I'm awake or not.

And I am never awake.

The Robin
perched atop the spruce
declares morning.

I become scarce—

nowhere near
young or open
or found.

The mirror's bloom,
this old face,
this gray plumage.

The Robin sings
her strong language
of air
for the breathless.

I am weary of her lyric.

My cloistered mind
always jumps
to cursing.

The coffee brews,
I become—

A crooked finger,
A short arm,
An aching bone.

A mind
without a bird.

Crows

When I saw them approaching
I believed
they were human

but really
they were hats
with twisted hands holding torches—

and then someone
somewhere spoke
about a "murder
of crows" erupting
before the sun rose
red over the ruined city
and I knew—

this is how the world
flies apart

this is how
the winds blow back

against the eagle building
her nest in a barren tree

and how
the hatted hands
torch
the tree's dry bark

but really
if you think about it

it's not about kneeling

or reporting

it's all that clawing
all that squawking

it's about the crows
and how they morph
into murders.

Rural Oregon. Tuesday. In September

Someone is burning garbage in a barrel.
The odor mingles with bacon, cut grass, roses.

An early breeze
lifts the edges of the table cloth.

The cat rolls
in a sunspot on the carpet,
a black bowling ball with yellow-eyed finger holes.

Out back
a doe munches an apple near the creek bank.

After such a dry summer, the creek is rocks.

The girls chatter
about clothes or boys

they drown out CNN.

My father calls from Arizona,
"We are under attack. Is your T.V. on?"

My girls flank me.

The dawn,
shining through the crystal candy dish,
detonates a kaleidoscope on the living room wall.

Outside
the doe leaps over the creek and bolts into the forest.

My father, "We are at war."

The cat
in her sunspot, nothing makes her happier.

What Now for April?

Rain
waters cactus
flowers in stone
cups, drowns
sparse grass.

Spring brings
no renewal,
recalls only
dead leaves,
forgotten Easters,
leftover ham
on a bare table,

a dying lily—

inside
the church exhales
swirling gospels,
thirsty hymns,

while a high
sky fans out
its bible for the sun.

Cleaning Out the Childhood Closet

She finds an etching
of the house when it was
young

frameless

smeared black
lead

tear stained buttery paper

with a frowning sun.

The house tries
to look painted
tries

to hide
the stick figure
peering out from its main
window

but she sees the girl
with her flippy hair,
her long lashes brushing
against streaky glass,

her
zig zagged lips
and triangle body
and curvy arms.

In the treeless yard
lush, tall grass
grows webby gray

around a giant lawn mower

and a bleeding red
gas can

another stick figure
                        also giant
bends and

reaches for the handle
with its clawed, crooked fingers.

She sighs,
looks around
the soulless bedroom,
wonders at its idyllic emptiness
wonders at how
it never possessed
even half a heart

She sighs

folds and pockets the etching,
fingers a cheap Bic lighter
held in her other hand
she shuts her eyes
blocks out the room
the house
the yard-view
out the broken window

Then one last time
she sighs
opens her eyes
reaches down
and grabs the waiting gas can.

Trimming the Rose Bushes 1973

They die quiet
the roses
in midsummer

even those
living in the shade
shrivel crispy
crumble noiseless
in Daddy's hand.

From a vinyl
spinning
inside the cabinet
that holds our family's faces
Lynn Anderson begs
us for pardons.

I sway back and forth
Listen to Lynn sing
about how we all
need a little rain

but here
in the desert
the sun shines
all the time.

Daddy hums along,
frowns at the browning
bushes he prunes.

I watch and think about smiling
and how the word "jolly"
reminds me of Christmas.

"What does 'melancholy' mean?"
I ask him.

He sighs
cups a withered rose

"This.
It means this."

Birth Day—Part One

What outlandish love
the way you bombarded me.

Your ear to my chest, listening
as though still inside.

And we slept that way
for hours after.

Before you, I longed for you
and all your chaotic beauty,
all your helpless need. And I wanted—

want

nothing more than to hold
you, your hand, forever.

The Afterlife Is a Dining Car

Prepare yourself,
the light says,
 a train comes.

I stand in the middle of the track.

The sky, in all its dreadful beauty,
Fills up with steam,
dust, papers in the train's wake.

Against daybreak the whistle blows.

Here it comes.

Is there really some great god
that will magic me up
in the gasp before impact and spirit
me into the dining car
where a last supper is all prepared
and waiting for me, where
the Holy Grail holds
the long lost elixir of everlasting life?
And I can drink my fill?

I believe fullness is my future.

But the brief millisecond between
breath and death is no sigh into the afterlife.

Here it comes.

Should I leap away?
Can I leap away?

I ask the light.

Prepare yourself,

-/-

passengers
feast on
candied apples,
honey hams,
lobster, duck a l'orange
with sugar snap peas,

bird-beaked children,
peck at grapes, cherries, spit
pits onto the plate

of an ancient woman, whose
hair holds moth balls, she
picks her teeth
with a knife.

-/-

The light assures me
You are not dead,
but awake
in a field
somewhere in Ohio, your bed
moved there years ago

The train slows
and I see a hill rolling
over a field of bluebells and
a maple holding the four poster,
complete with a robin's nest

the eggs gone.

The train stops, a crow
lights on my head, drops
a ticket into my hand, with words—

No expiration date

embossed in golden script.

I step down, look
at the tree bed, *how
am I going to get up there?*

the light answers,
fly.

Binary

We've been around for eons
trapped up here

where

I live as your shadow
or at best
an edge
to your age

circling you

I can see
how close you are to igniting,
how close to flaring

up

so

go ahead
go nova

I will absorb all
your screamy wreckage,

all your leaky H

until I become your
wild purple nimbus

breathing in
the best of your helium.

She—Continued

7. Puberty

She looks at herself
in the mirror and sees
the bumps and nipples
growing on her chest.

Her sister laughs as she wraps
the Ace round and round
She scowls at the hair
growing in private places.

The days of pretending are over.

On the bus the boy
who used to think she's a boy
ignores her,
unforgiving of her betrayal.

The girls
in the back whisper
about buying bras
giggle in her direction
while she picks
at the bindings under her T-shirt.

8. Original Sin

She hates
being all things girl.
She hates blossoming.
She is not a blooming rose,
a rough ruby.
She is not in God's image.

She is the product of original sin,
the cast off from Eden,
the everlasting comeuppance
of the apple.

Marked

My skin is clammy
where you touch it

everywhere

and this moist, muggy night
chokes me
when I try to suck it
through the straw
stuck in the tequila
bottle on the nightstand.

You and me—

we head bang
a waterbed baptism
to "Rebel Yell"
as the orange moon
drips
down on us

while
all the while
I tongue
wounds on your chest

and try to bite your heart out
to keep it mine.

Night Shift Musings in the Desert Southwest—Circa 1995

Beneath the fluorescent lights the numbers
are stacked
and sorted with batch clips.
The procedures are stripped of words
the near-dead have no names.

My fingers cackle the keys
on the cinder-block keyboard
and green fulsome numbers string
the monitor.
I enter and enter.

My daughters
meanwhile
sleep among mermaids,
in a room of underwater castles,
with a bubble machine that sings
lullabies.

What sun exists? Where?
Is it on the living room wall?
The kitchen counter?
Do my daughters know it?
Do they see a cactus
shadow-dance through
the window blinds?
They must have by now
learned the truth
about clapping for fairies,
and roads of yellow bricks
leading through looking glasses.
Do they know about Alice?
Aslan? Wild things and where they are?

My daughters know nothing of lake muck,
and the monsters that live there.
My green-filtered childhood sun was Michigan.
It would set on the dock, the lake,
the wagon wheel gate.
They know the sun of Arizona,
it requires hats, glasses, block.
They swim in chlorinated lakes
and don't know
the feel of Michigan mud
squished between their bare toes.

Their feet are missing
something important.

The sun of my days shines
on the bottom of the world.
It no longer filters up my way.

My upside-down night,
so bright.
I block it out
with light-fast drapes
and foiled windows.

My daughters creep by my bedroom door.
I hear a wash of whispers,
one went to a birthday party,
one likes pink pony-holders,
and one lost two teeth.
Did the tooth fairy come?
Have they learned the alphabet song?
Are they watching a sunspot
spider-crawl up the wall?

I fall asleep to their humming.

Birth Day—Part Two

What brings you here
this day before emerging
out and over and through

I saw you first
in a mirror and then on my chest
and our eyes met

that's when i knew
loving you was eternal

Urgent Prayers

The weight
of years
scrawls a marquee
across my mother's forehead,
bends her back.

She hugs the wall
step after step
down the hall
with its hills
and hazards,

*I took my pills
early, this weather
is not good for me.*

She longs for a satin
bed, spring air
brushing fresh roses
on her nightstand,
dewy mornings.

*I'd rather comb
my own hair,
peel my own apples.*

she blames
the way her
breathing puffs out,
how her eyes
no longer see,
blames how she
feels the need
to shout out
her urgent prayers
while her hand
curls
shaking
around my arm.

Golgotha

Easter Sunday
I return to Golgotha
and find Jesus gone.

Mary is here,
Magdalene,
she whispers in my ear
*the cross has changed
tangled wires now
tie it to the city.* She points—
*look it's real,
but Pilate's sign, INRI, was stolen
when the Pagan church was burned.*

At noon, we walk
the Via Dolorosa,
look for blood stains
along the stone steps, the wounds
of the earth are now
polished souvenirs.

The City betrays all memory,
it fell—and fell—centuries ago.

Inside the Holy Sepulcher
old fires still burn
during Holy Week.

At copper sunset
Mary whispers—
*it was never beautiful,
Jesus is always gone.*

Halo Flash
    After Time Person of Year, The Silence Breakers

The woman
who comes in wearing
clear Christmas lights
over her exquisite
shoulders
is wise
fearless

the lights
are on blinker

each one
representing
her brain's
electromagnetics

each one
declaring
her body's allegiance
to those
off-camera.

She turns
reveals her sign
"We are the elbows"

then
the ingenious part-

the lights
draping down
her back
stop blinking
until she snaps
her fingers

that's when they all halo-
flash around her head
and she becomes holy,
a new Mary.

Point Lobos

We leaked out
to a world of choppy water,

where the sea
left us alone,
it had no time for us,
no wisdom.

we stood still
and tall on a scarp
while the waves below surged
and rained spray

until the sea dropped
back and away

and even though
we were bereft,
washed out

we became salt and air.

The Wrong Companion

I was told I'd find you here.

Here

where the angel breathes out
fog, her mouth an ornament
of stone.

She stands her
frozen ground,
her ice-glazed wings
span a pillared snowscape,

a grey-tombed
garden, granite companions
keeping airy vigil.

I lay down
close to your name
but there is no gentle bed here
no soft linen scent.

Who chose
this place for you?
Who chose
these companions?

All your white
lilies turned to bone,
dust a decade ago.

If you live here
I cannot stay.

Psalm 23

Lord of love: open me up. *I shall not want.*

Pierce my heart, obliterate all of me; I am gored.

You abandon me: I am blind, maimed, possessed; speak to me, voice of water.

Leave me. Iron-winged statue, incarnate faith:

Yea, though I walk; this death bed floats, rocks, *fear no evil;* I am pale.

You, great shepherd, usher me through the Valley; I trawl in your wake: I am your bread; your blood-red wine, pour me out.

Brief Hope

Even though
the cherry tree's leaves
are green with new May

I call out to air less pure

hear mourning
hiss through old phone lines

see bruised, shriveled apples dying
in a fractured bowl.

These walls are sour.

Will washing even matter?

A peeling back is required.

An acquaintance
with aged impurity.

This house holds so much decay.

Yet out back
the hydrangea sips
droplets of rain.

Theresa Hamman is a writer and poet who lives in La Grande, Oregon. Born in 1963 in Michigan, she moved with her family to Arizona when she was nine years-old. Unable to cope with the Arizona heat, she and her two daughters relocated to a small rural northeast Oregon town called John Day in 1998. Five years later, in 2004, she and her daughters moved to La Grande. In 2011, after being laid off from her small office assistant job, she decided to attend Eastern Oregon University to earn her Master of Fine Arts in poetry degree. She graduated in 2016. She then went for and earned her Master of Arts degree in English Literature at Mercy College in New York, graduating in 2020.

She teaches undergraduate composition and creative writing courses at Eastern Oregon University and Southern New Hampshire University as a part time adjunct professor.

Her poems can be found in the following: *The Tower Journal, Oregon East, basalt, The Paddock Review, Red Savina Review, Red Wheelbarrow, Red Hyacinth, Atomic Flyswatter* and *Nailed*.

Although she enjoys writing in all creative genres, her first love is poetry. She gets lost in its musicality and enjoys how it bends language to create new objects.

Humming the Thing is her second chapbook. Her first, *All Those Lilting Tongues* was published in September 2018 by Finishing Line Press.

www.ingramcontent.com/pod-product-compliance
Lightning Source LLC
LaVergne TN
LVHW041601070426
835507LV00011B/1236